Nan

Written by Abie Longstaff

Illustrated by Srimalie Bassani

Collins

3

sit

nan

4

sip

a nap

sit

sit

sit sit sit

tip tip tip

/n/

14

 Review: After reading

Use your assessment from hearing the children read to choose any GPCs and words that need additional practice.

Read 1: Decoding

- Ask the children to mime the following words as you read the pages, to check their understanding.

  page 5: **sip** page 6: **nap** page 7: **tap** page 11: **pat**

- Point to **sit** on page 4, allowing them to sound and blend out loud. Repeat for **nan**. Then turn to page 12 and encourage the children to blend in their heads, silently, before reading the words aloud.

- Look at the "I spy sounds" pages (14–15) together. Point to the nine balloon and say "nine", emphasising the /n/ sound. Ask the children to find other things that start with the /n/ sound. (e.g. *necklace, nest, (music) notes, nap, newspaper, (fishing) net, nurse, nan, (sewing) needle, (basketball) net*)

Read 2: Prosody

- Turn to pages 6 and 7 and encourage the children to read the pages with a storyteller voice.
  - Read page 6 in a quiet tone, then ask: Why did I use a quiet tone? (e.g. *because the children's nan is sleeping and quiet*) Ask the children to read page 6.
  - Read page 7, emphasising the onomatopoeic sound of the words. Ask: Did the words sound like someone tapping? Encourage the children to read the page with expression too.
- Encourage the children to read both pages, using a different tone for each.

Read 3: Comprehension

- Talk about times the children have seen someone have a nap, like nan, or times they have napped themselves. Talk about the things that might wake people up from a nap.
- Ask the children:
  - On page 10, why is the girl patting her lap? (e.g. *to get the dog to come and sit on her lap*)
  - On pages 12 and 13, what made the chair tip? (e.g. *the dog jumping*)
- Encourage the children to talk about what people like nan need when they have a nap. (e.g. *quiet, to be left alone*) Go through the book, identifying what made nan wake up.